T0146820

Rendering in Black

Rendering in Black

Jose F Bolet

Library of Congress Control Number:		2015906421
ISBN:	Hardcover	978-1-5035-6438-1
	Softcover	978-1-5035-6440-4
	eBook	978-1-5035-6439-8

Print information available on the last page.

Rev. date: 11/25/2015

To order additional copies of this book, contact:
Xlibris
1-888-795-4274
www.Xlibris.com
Orders@Xlibris.com
710237

DEDICATION

This book is dedicated first to God, for keeping me alive, and giving me the strength to work every day, to my wife Mary, who has shared with me the toughest moments in my life, and my children Samantha, Karina and John Paul Bolet. You all mean the world to me.

PREFACE

I love to be an artist, but I never thought of how challenging this career would be.

By the year 2008 the recession has depleted all our savings and the financial situation at home was really desperate. Up to that point I had been able to combine my career as an artist with my business profession as a real estate broker managing and owning an independent small real estate office.

In February 2008, however, a letter came from the local realtor association suggesting me to pay the owed fees or shut down the office completely. Not having any other option, I finally did close our business that month of February.

After that day of February 2008, and for the next 4 years, I did work on whatever I could find to make money. From tax preparer to landscaper, freelance tree cutter, to foreclosure advisor, I also had a part time bookkeeping business that never got off the ground. Nothing seemed to help enough. I couldn't keep up with the expenses and Tired of going from one dead end job to another I decided to make a radical change.

In 2012, by following my friend and neighbor's suggestions I decided to get the CDL (Commercial driver License), which I finally got in November of that year. This CDL meant for me a great deal of stress and challenges that will test my motivation and determination to succeed on an activity that I felt intimidated, and was completely estranged and new for me.

There was nothing really bad or terrible about trucking, but my feelings were telling me something different. I was just about to change my whole lifestyle, my schedule, my life in general. I certainly was in need of money, but this wasn't for sure what I had in mind.

After some research and many days thinking about this career change, I decided to take the challenge up and go for it.

Meanwhile, my artistic output was keeping a good pace. I was able to have three to four exhibits every year. But sales were nowhere to be found. I was painting with determination and passion to succeed. Nonetheless, I was very aware that this new adventure would certainly make a stop on my production.

Before getting into the trucking school, I asked my neighbor to take me with him in one of his trips, so I could see and have an idea of how the job will be. He gladly accepted. So, in July, my whole family was waving at me as I departed to my new adventure, full of hope, worries and fears.

We departed from Chicago to Los Angeles. Little did I know the life changing experience that was waiting for me a few days ahead. On the morning of the third day we arrived very early to the destination, and after signing in, the receiver told us not to use the docks, but an isolated ramp on the side of the building.

My neighbor started to position the truck by the ramp so we could unload. I was behind the truck signaling him where to go. He stopped, got out of the truck to check the situation, and then he got in the truck again. At that point I was positioned between the truck and the ramp. He could not see me, and I wasn't able to see him. Without me realizing, my neighbor began to back up and in a split second, I found myself being crushed by the truck against the ramp. At this point it was only 6:30 in the morning. What a fantastic way to start my first expedition.

The truck was strongly pushing the air out of my lungs, I was unable to breath. No one was around. My neighbor kept backing, and with it, I felt as if I was about to be cut in half by the edges of the ramp. I was about to panic. My vision was blurred, and the lack of air in my lungs made it impossible for me to yell. I felt that with every second I was losing my life and close to death.

I couldn't think of anything. A few images of my family rushed through my mind. I was confused and puzzled by this unexpected event. How could this be happening?

My neighbor kept going backward completely unaware of what was going on behind the truck. With every inch backing, I felt more and more dizzy and the pain in my chest was almost unbearable. Suddenly he stopped, and when applying the air brakes the whole thing moved forward a few inches. I was then able to squish myself out and falling on the ground, I started to breathed. It was very difficult at the beginning because my lungs were compressed, but within a few seconds my breathing was getting normal.

No one noticed the incident and I did not say anything until the next day, when my neighbor asked me why I was so quiet? I told him what happened. He was shocked! We barely spoke the rest of the expedition.

After that incident, I spent weeks at home trying to make sense of that experience. I prayed and asked God for guidance and wisdom on what to do. I have been praying God to help me find a new job so I could restore our finances and ease the tension at home, and then, this happened. I was scared, and confused. I could have been killed that day!

Finally, by the month of September, and after a lot of thought, I I borrowed some money and entered the trucking school, graduating in November of 2012.

The whole 2013 year was spent driving an automatic Volvo hauling a 53' trailer all over the country. It was very hard at the beginning but little by little I was getting used to the hours, the schedule and the driving of this big rig.

On my first six months I was part of a driving team almost 24 hours a day. I drove by day and my partner during the night time. Traveling California to New York, Texas to Pennsylvania, East to West, North to South. We had very little spare time. We used to drive two, three weeks on a row, go home two or three days, and back on the road again. I was exhausted!

The memories of last year's incident were still fresh on my mind, but I did not allow them to stop me. I had a job and my family was happy that money was finally coming in regularly. I was in God's hands and that was enough for me.

It was on July, when I was given the opportunity to drive alone. This gave me a new perspective on my driving abilities and increased my spare time. I was able now to enjoy the wonders of this country and to take accounts of it's different landscapes, cities, monuments and people.

I then realized the great opportunity that was lying ahead of me. On January 2014, I took my drawing tools with me. I did not do anything for a month. The winter conditions, the snow, and the roads were enough to take my whole attention during the driving time, and by night, I was so exhausted, that I just wanted to sleep as much as possible.

February nonetheless, gave some relief since I was sent to work in states with much softer climates like North and South Carolina, Virginia, West Virginia, Kentucky, and some other southern states. That's when I started to get my drawing tools every time I could. I draw little things, people at the truck stops, interesting spots, landscapes and all that got my attention.

Back at home, in May, I bought a better, more adequate paper for finish drawing using pen, ink, pencil and marker. I began to be more selective of the chosen sites to draw and to take pictures of them, with the idea to work on the drawings later on.

These drawings became a habit and a great way to release the stress, finding joy and purpose on what I was doing. In order to get some feedback on the drawings, I started publishing them on Facebook, and surprise, I was getting great positive comments and many likes.

As the months went by, the drawings were getting more complicated, more detailed. I wanted to draw everything I saw; people, landscapes, buildings, texture, and the effects of light as a result of weather conditions. I was finding a new creating process and motivation, a new reason to see and feel with purpose.

These drawings, most of them in a small format, explore my interest in conveying mood and the relationship between the subject matter and the capture of all that seems essential about the subject itself. It also explores how I see things and how I express myself through line, values and form.

They do not pretend to be an exact representation of the location or even a precise rendering of the subject. They do though; pretend to depict an intimate relationship with the subject and my own view and interpretation of the landscape in front of me.

There is in these works a great concern and emphasis in line and values. They do not pretend to explore the full range of possibilities of the medium itself instead, they reveal the expressiveness of the most basic elements of drawings.

This book is the result of all that effort to not let circumstances to stop me, rather to use them on my favor. It is also the result of a great determination to succeed trusting on my God giving abilities, and a profound desire to make art that represents my unique vision about life.

It is also the result of my love and commitment to my family. Every time I go back home and see a smiling face on my wife and children, my heart gets fill with joy and satisfaction. I thank God every day for the opportunity to work, the strength and motivation to succeed.

I am grateful for the many wonderful people and friends I have met along this journey, that have supported me during this period of my life. Special thanks to Emanuel Cretu and his family, whose knowledge and generosity toward me and my family, made this career change possible. Also my special recognition to our friend Shireen Dim, for her unconditional support.

"Go on working. Freely and furiously, and you will make progress"

Paul Gauguin.

Winter Landscape, Crystal Lake, IL.
Very cold afternoon after the storm.

Strong, Elgin, IL

Spring in Mebane, Mebane, North Carolina

Afternoon by the Fox River, Algonguin, IL

Forrest. Avila Mountain, Caracas, Venezuela.

Drawing based on a photo provided by my Friend Helios Zapata,
taken in the Avila mountain, Caracas Venezuela

Barrington Lake, Barrington, IL

Fall afternoon in Arlington Heights, Arlington Heights, IL

Island in Fox River, Elgin IL.
Relaxing weekend walking alone by the river.

Old Court House building, Woodstock, IL

This magnificent building used to be a prison, and after remodeling,
it is now one of the cultural centers of Woodstock, IL

Woodstock Square, Woodstock IL

This is one of my favorite towns to go visit when I am home. It has a great cultural center and the square is just across the street from the Old court house building.

Cold afternoon at the Eddison train station in Chicago. Chicago, IL

This drawing was done on site. I was dropped from work at the train
station to go home, when I got so impressed by the place and its
enigmatic view. It reminds me of those horror movies in rural places. It
was very cold, and windy. I had to draw it from inside the station.

Parking lot in Mebane, North Carolina.

Solitude,

This drawing was done from memory and it may be a
recollection of different places put together.

Fall Landscape, Cary, IL.

When taking the picture to work on this drawing, a lady came to me very
curious about what I was doing in this private property. I told her I was
an artist and that this photo was material for a painting or a drawing I
wanted to do. She was surprised by my answer, and walked away

Vanessa's World.

My niece Vanessa on meditation by the river. She is a
lawyer with a great feeling for nature.

The Bird.

I thought this would be an interesting study of nature.

The black road, Barrington, IL

I love the different textures and techniques I used on this drawing.

House by the Road. Algonguin, IL

One day, I had just dropped my wife at work, when I saw this house. I felt
prompted to stop and take a picture with my phone. I was impressed by the scene,
the house, and the fact that it is very close from home, but I never noticed.

The abandoned house, Crystal Lake, IL

The visit.

This happened early morning. They were all over the road
and some of them ran to the nearest houses.

Landscape in Kingman, Arizona.

The Country club in late afternoon, Barrington, IL.

This drawing was done with watercolors and just very few strokes of ink.

Storm approaching, Sleepy Hollow, IL.

Dawn in L.A., los Angeles, California

Working this day since 3:30am, I saw this beautiful landscape in front of me.

Study of forrest

Drawn from memory.

Printed in the United States
By Bookmasters